The N~~iss~~ ... ~~tective~~ ve Mike

First edition November 2009

First Published Great Britain 2010
by Summertime Publishing

ISBN 978-1-904881-20-9

Printed by LightningSource

Designed by Felipe Torniziello

To our children Linus, Sofia, Francesca, and Fausto

Table of Contents

Acknowledgements

During our experience as expatriates, we have met many families having serious adaptation problems. Their difficulties in helping their own children, as well as their struggle to convince international schools and sponsoring companies that their families needed special attention, and sometimes professional support, have been a source of motivation for us in the process of writing this book. We want to thank those families for their contribution.

A special thanks to Debora West, a very sensitive and kind ESL teacher, for her collaboration and insights about the emotional needs of pupils who cannot communicate when they first arrive in a new school.

We are also very grateful to our illustrator Meri, or Maria Isabel Vaz Guimarães, and Evely Armando for their trust and enthusiasm. Our gratitude goes as well to our publisher, Jo Parfitt, for her patience and guidance in making this book clearer and more child-friendly.

Finally, we also want to thank our husbands, Carlo and Ulf, for their unconditional support.

Simone and Ana

Who this book is for

The way a child perceives international transition and adaptation is different from an adult. A child is confronted by specific difficulties and fears depending on the stage of emotional and cognitive development in which he or she finds him or herself at the time. The impact of the successes and failures of expatriation on a child can last for a lifetime.

Until now, most intercultural training for children has been based on the training programs created for adults. Unfortunately, the child's developmental stage and cognitive limitations have not been taken into account. Neither have the parents' emotional status or the family's previous international history been considered. Moreover, references to a child's individual intercultural readiness are lacking as is matching between home-culture and culture at the destination. The result has been a superficial 'cut & paste' strategy without any specific psychological foundation.

The objective of this book is to provide a tool for parents, educators and mobility professionals before, during and after an international assignment. Because parents and teachers become a child's main source of support during transition, their understanding and ability to discuss his or her issues openly and appropriately can be decisive. We believe that international schools' welcome procedures should be based on psychological research. Mobility professionals, responsible for the practical problems of relocation, the 'hard problems', could also benefit from taking a closer look at what often lies at the heart of family distress: the child's emotional well-being. To be sure, the latter directly impacts a child's ability to adapt, which, in turn, affects their employee's performance. Since HR professionals hire intercultural training programs, they should also be aware of the important issues that should be included in family (and children's) training. This book strives to address these needs.

Empirical observation of a group of children in an international school in Italy, as well as my experience as a psychologist and intercultural coach, confirmed the impression that parents and teachers tend to underestimate children's difficulties. This group of students was a good example of children who, typically, do not participate in the decision to move. Usually, parents have not been specifically trained to deal with the transition period, nor do they know what the long-term impact is on a child's development or on family relations. Consequently, they are not able to offer an explanation in a language to which their children can relate.

In the adult's world, where the challenges of globalization and expectations about international experiences predominate, a child´s fears and challenges often go unnoticed. Due to a lack of awareness, my patients and their families have often been faced with difficulties that may last a lifetime, even if the child does not show academic problems that affect her or his grades.

We, the authors, hope this book will create awareness in adults in companies, schools and families, who are responsible for important decisions regarding expatriation, that a child's perception of moving is typically concrete and egocentric and should be understood and dealt with in an appropriate way. By better understanding their perceptions, we, adults, can fill in the gaps with information children need but seldom know how to ask for.

This book would not exist without the talent, sensibility and ability of Ana Serra to transform psychological concepts into concrete facts in a language appropriate for children. Oftentimes our discussions were related to our own personal experiences as expatriate women (in intercultural marriages), and mothers who were just trying to understand and help our own children (Francesca, Sofia, Linus and Fausto, nine, nine, fifteen, and seven, respectively). Today, our children are called 'third-culture kids' (TCKs), referring to children who move constantly into other cultures; who, voluntarily or not, follow their parents on international assignments. Through their often difficult experiences, our children have taught us to validate and respect their feelings, fears and their innate search to belong, have friends and overcome limits to flourish in a healthy and happy way. For more information on how this book can be used as a tool in the overall process of expatriation visit www.interculturalplus.com.

Chapter 1

Moving: Leaving Something Behind?

"Pssss, pssss, pssssss . . ."

Why are my parents always whispering?
It sounds like they're speaking another language.

"Pssss, pssss, pssssss . . ." What are they saying?
What's going on? Are we being invaded by Martians or
something? Mike wondered about a lot of things.

Did I hear my name? Mike listened more carefully as
he went to the kitchen for an apple. The words he was able
to make out, "we have to move," were stamped on his mind.

Move, moving, moving out . . . What does that mean?
He was determined to find out. He looked it up in his dictionary.

"M . . . mmm . . . ma, me, mi, mor, move! To change place or position.
Change, leave something behind. Exchange one thing for another," he read to
himself. Hmmm . . . I wonder what's going to change in the house, he wondered. Maybe we're
changing the way we speak too and from now on we'll just whisper and say pssss, pssss, and
pssss?

What's being moved to another place? Our dog? Because he ate Daddy's slippers? The place in
the kitchen where the biscuits go? I won't be able to reach them anymore. Or . . . Me? Nooooo!
How confusing it all was for Mike. He was really scared. So many questions went through his
mind that the expression on his face changed.

Mike's parents knew they needed to explain what was going on. He would be turning nine shortly
and would certainly understand.

Their news had nothing to do with a Martian invasion or hiding the biscuits; it was actually an
adventure. Within a few months they would be living somewhere else.

His father's job was different from all the other fathers' jobs. He was not a shop owner who was
always in his shop. He was not a policeman who took care of the neighbourhood or a doctor at the
Medical Centre where Mike went when he was sick.

His father always talked on the phone in other languages, had countless meetings and travelled to different countries, sometimes staying away from home for a long time.

Mike's father explained that he had to work for a while in another place, and, in order for the family to be together, they would have to leave their house and live somewhere else.

After talking to him, Mike's face changed. The question mark on his forehead became smaller and was replaced by lots of exclamation marks. A sad smile grew on his lips.

He sat under his favourite tree and started thinking about his friends, his school, his toys.

He had thousands of questions: What's this new place like? Where are we going to buy candy? Are there playgrounds? Ice cream? And what about my things? And my house? And, and, and . . . So many thoughts crossed his mind that he felt like it would explode.

"I know," he said, picking up his walkie-talkie. "I'll talk to my friend Ikem about it."

"1 . . . 2 . . . 3 . . . Mike calling. Over."

"3 . . . 2 . . . 1 . . . Ikem here. What's going on? Over."

"Hello there. We have a new mission. Over."

"Roger. Let's meet at the tree house after we do our homework. Over."

"Roger, Roger. I'll bring the chocolate biscuits. Over and out."

That afternoon, Mike told his friend all about his news.

"That's it. We're going to live in another place. I know a lot of things will change, but I don't know how, and that's why I need your help." He threw up his hands helplessly and reached for another biscuit.

"You can count on me! We'll solve this mystery together."

"We're not the best detectives at our school for nothing!" they shouted before giving each other a high five.

What's the new place like and what can children do there? Those were the first mysteries Detective Mike and Ikem would have to solve on this new mission.

They hung up a huge world map in the tree house to find the mysterious city his parents had spoken about. But they couldn't find it anywhere. The world is so big!

"We need to look for more clues," said Ikem.

"Let's check the library in my house. We have so many books. We even have an atlas where Daddy shows me all the countries he travels to," suggested Mike.

They spent hours in the library, reading incredible stories about extraordinary places and different-looking people who lived far away. They saw thousands of colourful maps. There were mountains, rivers, deserts and cities, so many cities with weird and funny names, like that city in Mexico called Chihuahua (yes, like the tiny dogs), but nothing about this small, unknown city his family was moving to. They would have to ask Mike's parents for more information.

"As Sherlock Holmes would say, 'elementary, my dear Watson!'" said Mike thinking about his father's collection of the famous detective's mystery books.

His parents explained that the city they were moving to was located on another continent and was famous for its history. They also said it was located in the southern region of the highest mountain in that nation. That was enough for the famous detectives to immediately find the correct spot.

Great! The city was not so small, and according to the map, not far from the coast and near a bigger city, quite a famous one.

Surfing on the Internet, they found out that a different language was spoken in this place, and that in the winter it was so cold it snowed (brrr) and to stay cool during the hot summer there were beaches nearby (splash). They also discovered a zoo where kids could care for newborn animals (awesome) and that the oldest buildings were built by the Romans (wow).

The friends agreed that Mike's grandpa, who used to be a teacher, could tell them more. He knew everything, could fix anything that was broken and, best of all, told the most incredible stories about his trips around the world.

19

"Of course, I know this city," exclaimed Mike's grandpa. "It was autumn when I visited. I don't remember the year - it's been a while - but I can still remember the pathways full of brown and yellow leaves and all the kids running through them to hear them crunch."

"Were there any playgrounds?" asked Mike.

"Yes, in the famous main square there was a playground with monkey bars, swings and a paved area for rollerblading and cycling competitions."

"What about ice cream?" asked Ikem concerned.

"Really delicious ice cream of all flavours. I used to have the biggest cone with five different scoops . . . mmmm . . . I can still taste it."

"Did you go to school there, Grandpa?" asked Mike, feeling a little insecure.

"No, I was much too old to go to school, but not too old to teach in one. I met a lady called Miss Luci, who used to teach at one of the funniest schools I've ever known."

"Why was it so funny?"

"Yes! Why? Tell us, Grandpa!" Mike shuffled in his seat to get comfy. He loved Grandpa's stories.

"In Miss Luci's class, kids started the day with a game called 'a world of friends'. They would write a letter to a child from another place. Little by little, they made a chain of friends all over the world and were introduced to different ways of living, eating, speaking and having fun."

"Wow! Brilliant! I guess my new city is a special place," replied Mike happily.

"Keep going, Grandpa. Tell us more," said Ikem, enjoying himself even though he wasn't going there!

Grandpa decided to show them some photos of his trip so they could see what the people and the city looked like.

Mike's new life was becoming more interesting. But too many questions still needed an answer and there were lots of things to be discovered. Besides, he was happy in his own city. He knew his way to the park. He already knew everyone in his school. He could even walk all the way to school and to his friends' house all by himself. In the new place, he would have to start all over again.

21

Our detective friends were glad to discover more about the new city (which wasn't a mystery anymore!) and, especially, what the children did there. However, they had to solve a new riddle: what was going to happen to Mike's things when they moved?

If moving also meant leaving something behind, like the dictionary said, were they supposed to leave their things and change them into other things?

"Oh, no! I won't change any of my lab experiment kits or the posters of my favourite team. Not over my dead body. I won't change them. I am not moving," moaned Mike.

"Take it easy. A detective never gets nervous. A good detective analyses the scene, looks for clues and solves the problem," said Ikem, a serious look on his face.

Mike knew that Ikem was right, but it wasn't easy to think like a detective when his things were at stake: his Nintendo DS, his duvet with the Interspatial Robot characters on it, his stickers and his football shirt signed by the team.

As the two friends were thinking and analysing all the information, a little girl was sitting in the garden crying. It was Lisa, Mike's sister who was five-years-old, but, in Mike's opinion, always acted like a baby!

"Hey, what's going on? Why are you crying?" they asked. Even boys could be caring sometimes.

"Because . . . sniff, sniff . . . because . . . because . . . sniff, sniff . . . because Mum said we're going to live somewhere else, and I don´t know what's going to happen to my dolls, my little houses, my colouring books, my costumes and . . . sniff, sniff . . . I'm going to end up without anything . . . waaah." Lisa's sobs were turning into big wails and she was wiping her nose on the skirt of her pretty dress, making it yucky.

The problem was more serious than they had thought. They simply had to find a solution as soon as possible; otherwise, they'd go deaf from Lisa's screaming and crying.

"Let's take a look at the clues," Ikem suggested. "Your garage is full of empty boxes. For the last couple of days, your mum has been separating things, packing up some things and throwing away so many others."

"Sniff . . .she's going to throw away all my dolls."

"No, she won't. Mum knows how much we like our things; she would never throw anything away!" explained Mike. "Maybe they'll be stored here until we get back?"

"No! I want my toys . . . sniff."

25

"I want my things too, Lisa; I don't want to be without them either."

"Wait a minute, guys. Let's make a plan so you won't lose your toys or your favourite things," suggested Ikem, taking a notebook out of his pocket along with a stubby pencil, the tip of which he now licked.

The three friends went to the garage and started going through the things Mike's mum was packing. The boxes were huge; they were made of wood and cardboard. Curiously, they climbed up a chair to look inside the biggest box. Oh, no! The chair tipped over, and they fell into the box.

They heard steps coming closer to the boxes. Who could it be? The movers? A thief? How frightening! Nobody knew they were there, so nobody could help them!

They heard boxes being moved and things being packed in bubble wrap. They were so frightened, they couldn't even move. Only their eyes moved from side to side, trying to find out where all that noise was coming from.

Suddenly, a familiar voice brought them back to reality.

"Kids, where are you?" called Mum.

"Here we are," they screamed, standing up inside the big box.

"Oh! You scared me out of my wits!" Mike's mum clapped her hands to her cheeks in surprise. "What are you doing here? I've been looking for you everywhere. I wanted to ask you to help me organise the toys."

"No, Mum. We don't want to leave our things behind. We don't want to exchange them for other things . . ."

"You don't want . . . What are you talking about? We're not leaving anything. Your things are coming with us, although they'll be taking a longer and more complicated trip."

They invited Mum to the tree house so she could explain what that trip would be like. She went for some biscuits and chocolate milk, and, as soon as she got to their special place, she made some drawings full of details and arrows on it. Mum showed them how they would be travelling and then how the boxes with all of their belongings would be arriving.

"We're travelling in a big plane, which will take us straight to the new city. The trip will be long but fun because sometimes there are TVs in the planes. There might even be video games," explained Mum.

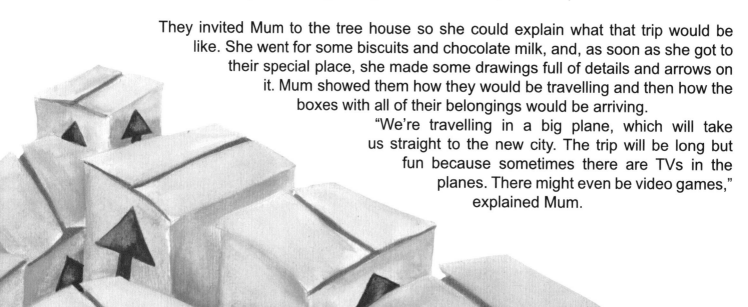

"Brilliant," said Mike. He liked the idea of watching a film on the plane.

"Our things will take longer because they'll travel by ship. They'll have to wait in the harbour for a while to be checked before being allowed into the new country."

"So we won't have our things for a long time?" asked Mike.

Lisa sniffed loudly and Mum handed her a tissue. Mums were good at things like that.

"Take it easy, guys. I've analysed all the clues. Did you know you're allowed to take your favourite things in your hand luggage? You know, the one bag you can take on the plane with you?" asked Ikem.

"Elementary, my dear Watson!"

Now calm and happy, Mike and Lisa ran off to their bedrooms to start separating those things they would carry on the plane and the others that would be shipped later on.

"What a tearful mission that was," Ikem said shaking his head. "I'm not sure girls should be allowed to come with us on the next one."

27

Chapter 4
Who Will Disappear?

One morning Mike woke up thinking about what was going to happen. He realised that they had forgotten something else. It was another important mystery they had to solve right away.

What would happen to his friends when he was gone? Mike remembered that, after his neighbours moved away, he never saw them again. It seemed as if the earth had swallowed them. Would the same thing happen when he moved? And the boy he used to meet at the bookstore on Saturdays? Mike never saw him again. Will I be alone? Will I disappear, too? he wondered. He reached for his walkie-talkie.

"1 . . .2 . . . 3 . . . Emergency, emergency. Over."

"3 . . . 2 . . . 1 . . . What's going on, Mike? What's the emergency? Over."

"Emergency meeting. Emergency! Do you copy? Over."

"Roger. Copied that. I'll see you at the tree house. Over and out."

Mike quickly climbed up to the tree house and started screaming and talking nonsense. He paced up and down, shaking his head and screwing his hands into fists.

"I'm here. What happened?" Ikem came rushing up the ladder.

"My friends, your friends, us! What's going to happen?"

"Calm down. I can't understand anything you're saying! What's going on?" He sat down on the wooden floor and pulled Mike down to sit beside him.

"I was thinking and realised that I don't know what's going to happen to my friends. It's a big mystery. Are they going to disappear? Will they forget about me? Will I forget their faces? Are they leaving, too? Is our friendship going to end? Will they erase my name from their memories?"

Suddenly, a cold silence took over the tree house. The only sound they heard was the far-away laughter of children at the playground.

"This is really serious," Ikem remarked, breaking the deafening quiet.

Both friends started thinking about what would happen when they would not be able to see each other everyday.

"I'm sure I'll forget everyone's face," Mike said putting his own face in his hands.

"Yes, you're right. Maybe we'll grow up so much we won't recognise each other anymore."

31

"What if they pick someone else as goal keeper instead of me? When I get back. . . they won't play with me anymore!"

"Take it easy. Anyway, we don't know if this'll happen. We'll have to solve this mystery."

Their first move was to ask Mike's parents if they still had childhood friends. They said they did, but only a few good friends because some had moved away. Others had different interests, so they just grew apart.

This first bit of information didn't help much, but it gave him hope that it was possible to remember old friends. Next, they went to the park and looked for the old couple that was always there, taking care of their grandchildren. They told great stories about their childhood and the games they played with other kids. They remembered all their childhood friends really well and could still describe them to this day.

They all laughed about the story of Mr Juan, who enjoyed talking about his adventures with his friend Luigi, the Big Ear, and Antonio, who used to split his pants every time he sat down. He also told them about Laura, the red-haired girl who used to cry more than anyone in the whole city. They felt better after finding out that the faces of friends were not forgotten, not even after one hundred years!

Their next move was to call an emergency meeting with Mike's friends from the neighbourhood: Clara and Sara, the two inseparable friends who had the best grades in school and Jack, who was really into computers. Only together would they be able to come to solve this mystery.

They met in the tree house, but there were more children than it could hold. The wood was creaking . . . creak, creak, creak . . . so they stood as still as possible when they began the meeting.

Mike told his friends about his concerns and suggested that each one of them give an opinion about what would happen to their friendship.

Some of them were so worried that their eyes filled with tears. Some laughed nervously when they heard that their friend might disappear. Clara, who was always kind and positive, said she wasn't at all worried about Mike moving away. She was pretty sure she would never forget him, and whenever she missed him, she would call him, just like she did when she missed her aunt who lived in another state.

"Elementary, my dear Watson," said Ikem.

"That's it. Yesss! I know what to do so we won't forget each other. I'll send emails about what we're doing in the new place."

"My sister has a boyfriend who's studying in Australia," said Sara excitedly. "They use Instant Messaging to keep in touch. We could do that, too."

"We have to promise to send lots of pictures so that we can see how we look as we grow up."

"We could also use Skype to talk online. My mum says it's a lot cheaper than calling on the telephone," suggested Jack, without looking up from his Gameboy. "I could even help you set up a blog."

"Cool! Great ideas! This way, we'll be friends forever, and I'll be able to show you my new city and introduce you to my new friends so they can be your friends, too."

"Wow! What a great idea. We'll have friends all over the world!" said Sara.

The children left the tree house carefully because the floor was creaking from the happiness of solving another mystery. The next day at school, they told their teacher about their plan. Jack asked if they could use the classroom computer to create a blog on the Internet that would be called "Kids of the Tree House".

The teacher was so impressed that she asked if they could do a report on their project for the entire class.

Chapter 5

The Mystery of the Mixed Up Tongue

Mike spent almost every day thinking about and preparing for the move. This week he started studying the new language he would be speaking with a private teacher. He hoped to speak a few words of the new language before they moved. But his tongue had a huge problem! It simply couldn't find the right position in his mouth to repeat the words the teacher was saying. At first he felt like laughing, but as the days passed, he started to worry.

"How will I ever understand the other kids and make myself understood? Each time I try to pronounce a word, my tongue twists and bends, and the weirdest sounds I've never heard come out of my mouth," he grumbled.

Mike's grandpa, who was often at his house since he lived in the same neighbourhood, was passing by his room when he overheard Mike telling Ikem about his silly tongue.

"Hey, I think I can help you," he offered, coming into the bedroom and sitting down on Mike's bed with the big whooping noise he always made when he sat down.

"Even you can't help me this time, Grandpa," Mike said hitting his forehead with the heel of his hand. "I can't change my body."

"Look, Mike, you just have a new mystery to solve. Do you remember what I told you about Miss Luci . . . that her students had created a game called 'a world of friends'? I think it would be nice for you to get to know those kids better."

"Grandpa, why do you think it's such a good idea? Don't you understand? My problem is that I can't talk to them. How do you think we'll be able to communicate if each time I want to say a word in this new language, my tongue gets wild and ends up saying nothing?"

"Hahahaha! This is not a problem, Mike. With a little practice, your tongue will do what you want it to do."

Mike thought his grandpa's intentions were good, but he still didn't think it was a good idea. Mum was always saying that practice made perfect, but come on, this time it was harder than ever. He'd never do it.

"OK," he said quietly. "I'll try."

Grandpa just looked at him as if he could read his mind.

Yeah, right, I'll try. Even though I don't think it'll work, he thought. Then, he heard more of Mum's words inside his head: "If at first you don't succeed, try, try again". She was right as usual. If it doesn't work, I can try something else. After all, I am a detective. I have to follow all the clues leading to the solution, right? Mike stood up ready for action.

37

And that's how they decided to contact Miss Luci´s students, through a 'chat room' on the Internet. Mike and Ikem were on one computer at home using a web camera and the kids from Miss Luci´s class were on their school computer. They all talked at the same time and it made a terrible noise.

The first day was a disaster. There were some kids in the Miss Luci's classs who spoke only to each other, and Mike hadn't a clue what they were saying. Miss Luci moved in front of the camera and apologised to Mike and Ikem in their language.

She promised that she would speak to the children about how to behave and they would try again later.

On the second day, things got more interesting . . . more pleasant . . . or more strange . . . Mike wasn't sure.

When the webcam went on, all the children at Miss Luci's went silent. They looked at Mike and Ikem curiously, observing every inch of the screen as if to discover something about them, without having to say a word. Mike and Ikem did the same. They sat in silence and just looked.

When the situation got too tense, because no one dared to speak, they waved goodbye to each other and switched off the computers.

It all seemed useless.

"I knew this wasn't a good idea! It was impossible to communicate. I will never be able to talk to anyone over there. Never. Well at least I know the truth now: I'm going to be alone, without any friends. Mum . . . I'm NOT MOVING ANYWHERE!"

Mike turned his face towards the open door and screamed as loud as he could. But no one heard him.

Mike was discouraged and convinced that his life at this new place would be unhappy because his tongue would never pronounce this strange language.

Focused on his own thoughts, he didn't notice that his sister Lisa wanted to say something. She had been there in the room with them all the time, sitting on the floor beside him and he hadn't even noticed. She had been trying to get his attention for more than ten minutes. Since he didn't answer her, she decided to draw a pizza, what she wanted to say was ´dinner's ready ´. Maybe that would get Mike's attention and help him to understand what she was saying?

That was when Mike had a brilliant idea.

"Why don't we invent a new way of communicating that we all understand? A good way to be understood until my mixed up tongue finds a way to pronounce the words properly?"

That's when Mike and his inseparable friend Ikem created a dictionary, which they called the "Dictionary for Tied Up Tongues".

They spent all afternoon cutting pictures out of magazines, taking photographs and drawing and painting until the dictionary was finally ready. They agreed to use it the next day to communicate with Miss Luci's students.

As soon as the computer was turned on, our friends' hearts were beating fast. They had devised the perfect way to communicate. The time to put it into action had come. This was the final test.

At first all the kids sat looking at the screen, speechless, just like the last time.

By smiling, drawing and mimicking, they managed, little by little, to communicate.

What a wonderful day! What a special moment! Mike, Ikem and Miss Luci's class were happy and proud of what they had achieved. Even Mike's tongue became untied and started to pronounce the words properly.

Yet again, the detectives had solved another inexplicable mystery, learned new words and came up with ideas to improve the dictionary. But, above all, they had made new friends.

The move had become a great adventure, full of mysteries to be solved and emotions to be felt. Moving didn't seem so sad anymore.

Mike was curious to see the new city and his new school. Every day he imagined what his friends would be like and wondered if his new teacher would be as pretty and nice as Miss Nancy, his current teacher.

Then, the word "NEW" appeared with big letters in his mind. After all, it would be nice to have new things. He always liked the smell of new clothes, the games he invented when he got a new toy and the excitement he felt when he learned something new at school.

But lately, the question marks (?) and exclamation marks (!) kept popping up, which almost always meant a new mystery was forming.

This time was no different. The great mystery had something to do with his house. "What's going to happen to my house?" he asked himself.

Mike's house was one of the most important places in his life, where he had lived meaningful moments, like building the tree house, learning to make chocolate candy with his mum, taking a nap with his dog, decorating the Christmas tree with everyone and so many other things.

NEW meant that, in his NEW HOUSE, everything would be . . . NEW, which might also mean DIFFERENT, STRANGE, UNKNOWN . . . and . . . without the moments that had made him happy in his current house.

"Oh, no!" he exclaimed out loud. "This can't be happening. How will I solve this mystery?" He scratched his chin. "I know . . . I'll ask Daddy if we can take our house with us. And what about the tree house? Can we take that with us? Will it fit on the ship?"

Mike spent all afternoon making and unmaking plans to find the best way to take apart his house, put it in a box and put it back together later, the same way it was, in their new city.

He spent a lot of time measuring, touching the materials, thinking, drawing and wondering, but he still could not find the right way to take the house.

When his father came home from work, Mike showed him his plans and calculations, to see if together they could solve the problem.

Mike's father looked at his plans very carefully and after thinking for a while (placing his index finger on his forehead, as he would do each time he had something important to say) said, "Son, I see you're working on a new case. I think I can help you."

"Yesss! I knew you'd figure out a way to take our house with us."

"Mike, what exactly do you like about our house?"

"I like it when we eat together and I tell you what I did at school and you tell me about your childhood. Hmmm . . . I like it when Lisa sings and dances and we're her audience. I like it when we fix the bike together in the garage. Oh, I also like it when Mum makes a picnic lunch for the tree house."

"My dear Mike, did you notice that everything you like about the house isn't really about this house; it's not related to the walls or the roof. What you're talking about are the good times and all the other

experiences we've shared inside the house?" His dad sat down beside him at the kitchen table and laid his hands on it. "It's not about this table. We just need any old table. Does that make sense?" Mike nodded. And now he began to think, placing his index finger on his forehead.

"Elementary, my dear Watson!" Mike had a brilliant idea. "We don't actually need to take the house; being together is more important. We can do the things we like to do anywhere and in any house. Like having one house that we can touch and see and another one that's invisible, where we do cool family things together."

"That's it Mr. Detective. You've got it. You really know how to solve a mystery! You've also learned the difference between a house and a home. We see a house with our eyes. A home we see and feel with our hearts. 'Home' is all the nice and cosy things we do as a family and make us happy inside. 'Home' is made of our family routines and nice moments. Our way of doing things will always be with us, wherever we go."

44

"So you mean that even without a house we can still have a home? Like when we stay at a hotel, waiting to move, right? So a home is invisible?"

"That's right. A good detective knows that there can be a home without having or even seeing a house."

"Brilliant, Daddy! Then we can build a new tree house together and do all the other nice things we've always done. We really don't need to make plans to take apart and move our house."

45

Chapter 7
The Abilities of a Real Detective

In the course of this story Mike has experienced many moments filled with fears, tears, curiosity and laughter. Above all, in order to solve the mysteries, he has used a bit of wisdom, imagination and some help from his family and friends.

Even though he has learned that moving brings many new, good, different and surprising experiences and, especially, more cases to be solved, he has mixed feelings. Sometimes he´s all excited about the moving and sometimes he´s sad about leaving his pals and a bit nervous about the new school and making new friends.

Anyway, today is a special day for Mike: he is travelling in a huge plane and in a moment will arrive in his new city. Looking out of the window just before landing, he sees the city, playgrounds and houses. Which one is his? He keeps looking, thinking and looking again.

Lisa has also been curious, so much that she argued with Mike over who would sit next to the tiny window.

"Look over there. Oh, how beautiful! Look at that big playground next to that big building. Could that be our school? Wow! Mum, can we play there? Can we? Oooh! Let's go for a bike ride there, Mike. Come on, come on, can we?"

"Lisa, shut up. Try to be quiet for a minute, would you? I can't see anything," yells Mike, angry with his sister, who just won't let him look out the window in peace.

When they leave the airport, they take a taxi and drive a long way to get to a huge white house.

"Mum, is this our new house?" asks Lisa.

"No, this is the hotel where we'll be living for the next few weeks until our furniture arrives. Do you remember when we were packing all the boxes and I told you about the trip our things would take?" Mum says, taking Lisa's hand in hers to make her feel safe. She looks over at Mike.

"Oh, yes." Mike nods, suddenly remembering what he had learned just a few weeks before. "They're taking a longer trip because they're coming by sea. Sure, there are so many and heavy things that if they came with us, the plane would certainly fall from the sky. There wasn't any room in the car either," says Mike laughing a little at the picture he made in his mind of trying to cram everything they owned into a taxi.

49

After staying in the hotel for a few days, Mike realises he is having a lot of fun: jumping on the big beds, eating in the restaurant, swimming in the pool and watching TV in the bedroom. He thinks it is like living in the invisible house (or home).

Every day they walk around the city. They already knew where the best park is, the one with the rollerblading course and other cool things to do. They even discovered the ice cream parlour with huge ice cream cones that Grandpa had described.

Mike's first day of school is a bit tense to start with, but after a while, the teachers become very kind. The kids smile, but they also look at him with curiosity since it isn't easy to communicate. All those happy faces and friendly smiles make him feel better. He already has a friend who is called his 'buddy' though his real name is Cory. Cory is in charge of showing Mike around the school, so they are together all the time.

During that first week, their mum stays at school for a while so they – I mean his sister - would feel safe. Lisa won't let go of Mum's hand for a second!

During the break a few other classmates join them for a tour of the school. They go to the gymnasium, the music room, the art room and the computer lab.

One of the first words Mike learns is 'restroom!' Oh, no! His new friends have forgotten to show him where the restroom is and he needs to go – and in a big hurry.

He draws faces, signs, even looks for pictures in his "Dictionary for Tied Up Tongues". Then he realises he has never thought of a picture for this particular situation.

Ali, one of his classmates who is also a foreigner, understands what Mike wants and explains it to the teacher. Luckily, he's also been in this situation before, so he runs to the restroom with Mike, so fast that for many months, the kids say they broke an Olympic record.

Mike talks to Ikem every single day using a web camera on the computer. He tells him about the city, his new friends, the exotic and delicious fruits they can buy at the supermarket. He teaches him how to pronounce the words he is learning. Ikem loves listening to his stories about school and wants to hear about what games they play and if they also collect stickers.

At last it is time to move in to his new house. He will finally see all his toys, his collection of Interspatial Robots stickers, his bed, his signed shirt, his duvet, his posters . . .

Oooh, it's so nice to be home again. Now we have a house and a home at the same place, he thinks.

Despite being so different, the new house is nice. There is a small garden and a lot of rooms. He feels happy, comfortable and relaxed inside the new house because he has everything he needs: his family, his things and a big tree to rebuild his secret place. What else can he ask for? This is his home, the way he wanted it to be.

Mike sits on his bed and looks at the mirror. Inside the mirror he sees his friend Ikem!? Don't worry, this isn't another mystery!

Inside the mirror Ikem, his imaginary friend, smiles at him and says hello. Slowly his image fades away.

Mike is not sad. His friend has helped him face lots of problems, and he knows that Ikem could come and help him whenever necessary. Ikem and the mysteries they had solved together will always be in his heart.

Now he is ready for new adventures in new places and with new friends. He has learned that even unknown and mysterious new things can bring good surprises. He has learned that even if we don't understand the adult world very well, we can always look for information and ask for help. He now knows that even if you don't see your old friends, they will not disappear (they're just invisible to our eyes, but not to our hearts), and that when learning a new language, making mistakes is part of the fun.

After all moving - changing place or position, changing, leaving something behind - isn't as terrible as he had thought; rather, it is an opportunity to open his world to new adventures.

About the Authors

Simone T. Costa Eriksson is a psychologist (member of the British Psychological Society) and intercultural coach based in Brazil. She also holds an MBA from Lund University, Sweden. Simone´s interest in the long-term impact of expatriation on executive performance and on family relations began with her own experience of 13 years abroad (USA, Sweden, Poland, and Italy), most of the time, as an expatriate mother with two children. Simone holds seminars and workshops for HR professionals, expatriate families and children, and for international schools. You can find out more at her website www.interculturalplus.com or email her on info@interculturalplus.com.

Ana Serra is a children´s poet and storyteller. In 2006, she was a finalist of the XIV Certame internacional "Nueva Literatura de Habla Hispana" Editorial Nuevo Ser when two of her stories were selected and published for the anthologies "Nueva Literatura de Habla Hispana". In 2005, she was a finalist of the Certame Internacional "Crisol Literário" when four of her works were selected and published as "Crisol Literário" by Editorial do Centro de Escritores Nacionais de Argentina. Ana graduated in cultural management from the Universidade Blas Pascal (Córdoba, Argentina) and has a degree in Marketing Communication from Instituto de Estúdios Superiores (IES 21, Córdoba, Argentina).

The Illustrator

Maria Isabel Vaz Guimarães´s nickname is Meri. Since she was a child she´s always dreamt of illustrating children´s books. She has an arts degree and since 2005 has illustrated 12 books, most of them using oil paint. Her creativity, talent and personal experience of moving 16 times during childhood contributed to an almost instant synergy with the authors and has added great value to this book.

What next?

Children, please email us to tell us:

- about how you felt when you moved abroad
- what new missions you want Detective Mike to solve
- about how you found your own solutions to his existing missions

write to: detectivemike@interculturalplus.com

55

CPSIA information can be obtained
at www.ICGtesting.com
Printed in the USA
2694LVUK00002B